Let's Talk About Pets

Raising Rabbits

David and Patricia Armentrout

ROURKE PUBLISHING

www.rourkepublishing.com

www.rourkepublishing.com

Photo credits: Cover © cameilia; Contents © Joshua Lewis; Page 4 © Alekcey; Page 5 © zeljkosantrac; Page 6 © jokerpro; Page 7 © HamsterMan; Page 8 © Sandra Blalock www.superior cages.com; Page 9 © Katrina Brown; Page 10 © Blue Door Publishing; Page 11 © Socrates; Page 12 © Mchudo; Page 13 © Lucky Business, muzsy, Istvan Csak; Page 14 © Alexnn; Page 15 © Coprid; Page 16 © naluwan; Page 17 © Nagy-Bagoly Arpad; Page 18 © muzsy; Page 19 © Monkeybusiness; Page 20 © Orion9nl; Page 21 © shellyagami-photoar; Page 22 © Perrush, Linn Currie, Elena Elisseeva, Csaba Vanyi, Linn Currie

Editor: Jeanne Sturm

Cover and page design by Nicola Stratford, bdpublishing.com

Library of Congress Cataloging-in-Publication Data

Armentrout, David, 1962-
 Raising rabbits / David and Patricia Armentrout.
    p. cm. -- (Let's talk about pets)
 Includes bibliographical references and index.
 ISBN 978-1-61590-249-1 (Hard cover) (alk. paper)
 ISBN 978-1-61590-489-1 (Soft cover)
 1. Rabbits--Juvenile literature. 2. Pets--Juvenile literature. I. Armentrout, Patricia, 1960- II. Title.
 SF453.2.A76 2011
 636.932'2--dc22
                            2010009849

Rourke Publishing
Printed in the United States of America, North Mankato, Minnesota
033010
033010LP

www.rourkepublishing.com - rourke@rourkepublishing.com
Post Office Box 643328 Vero Beach, Florida 32964

TABLE OF CONTENTS

RAISING RABBITS

You probably have friends who have pet dogs, cats, or both. Maybe you are looking for a special pet, too. Have you thought about a pet rabbit?

Just like dogs and cats, rabbits are smart, curious, and loving animals. They are also very social animals. So, if you are adopting one rabbit, consider a bunny buddy. You can raise two rabbits as easily as one!

Bunny Bonding

Spaying female rabbits and **neutering** male rabbits prevent unwanted babies. The operations also help rabbits live longer and healthier lives. Spaying prevents cancers in females. Neutering helps reduce aggressive behaviors in males. Both spayed and neutered rabbits have calmer personalities.

Female rabbits can reproduce three times a year and typically give birth to three to eight bunnies at a time.

The safest place to keep a pet rabbit is inside. An outdoor rabbit that cannot escape a predator can die from fright.

HOUSE RABBITS

Domestic rabbits need attention and special care from their owners. Pet rabbits kept outside are **isolated**. Experts recommend housing your rabbits indoors. This keeps your furry friends out of the rain and snow, and protects them from curious dogs and **predators** like raccoons.

DID YOU KNOW? . . .

House rabbits typically have an 8- to 12-year lifespan.

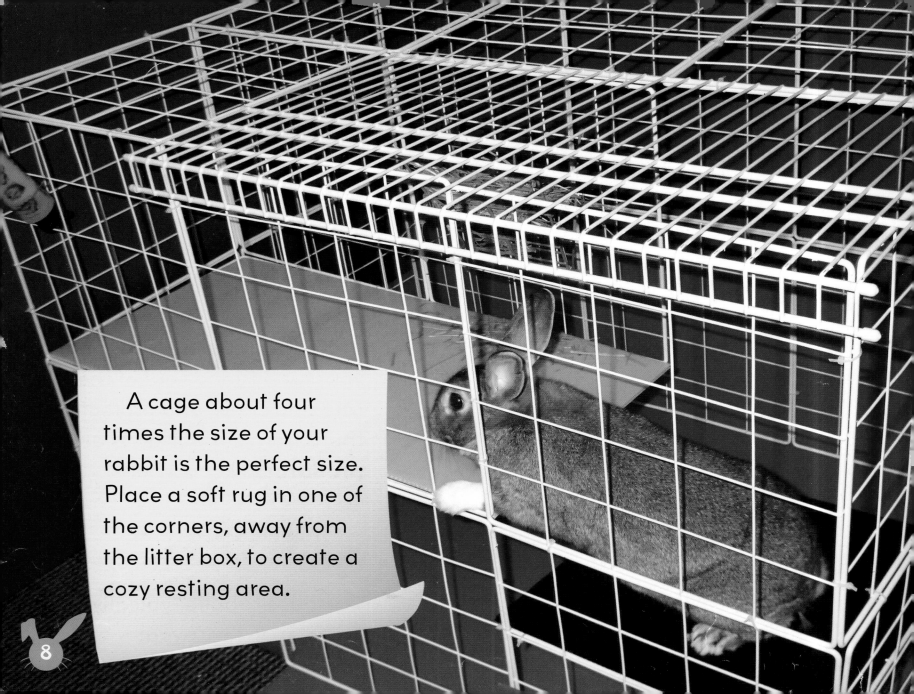

A cage about four times the size of your rabbit is the perfect size. Place a soft rug in one of the corners, away from the litter box, to create a cozy resting area.

Rabbit housing includes a multi-level cage. It's a safe space where your rabbits eat, sleep, and enjoy each other's company when you are not home. Place a food tray, water bowl or bottle, toys, and a litter box inside. (More about the litter box later.)

Housing should also include an exercise pen. A simple fenced area on the floor works well. You can buy a pen from a pet store or build one at home.

Some owners let their bunnies roam the house. Because rabbits love to chew on just about anything, it is best to make one room safe for your bunnies, or use an exercise pen.

You can use an outdoor exercise pen for your rabbit if the weather is mild. Make sure that your rabbit is safe from predators and harmful weeds.

EXERCISE AND PLAYTIME

House rabbits need space to hop and jump. At least two hours a day in their exercise pen is ideal. Balls with bells inside, wooden rings, and woven basket tunnels keep them occupied. Chew toys made from willow help keep their teeth trim. You can make cardboard tunnels so they can hide inside—rabbits love that!

DID YOU KNOW? . . .

Some rabbits learn to come when called by name, or perform jumping tricks for treats?

Natural chew toys are a good source of fiber in your rabbit's diet.

If you take your rabbit outside, use a collar and leash. Be sure to keep him away from plants and grasses that have chemicals or fertilizers on them.

11

DIET

Feed your pet rabbits plenty of good quality hay, such as timothy hay. **Supplement** their fresh hay diet with rabbit food **pellets**. Of course, your bunnies will enjoy treats every once in a while.

Diet Ideas

parsley

carrot tops

fruit

Fresh greens like parsley, carrot tops, and spinach are all great choices to supplement your rabbit's diet. Occasionally, you can give your rabbits a small amount of fruit, about 2 tablespoons (30 milliliters) for every 5 pounds (2.27 kilograms) of body weight.

Don't forget to provide clean, fresh water at all times. If your rabbits like to hop into and splash water out of a bowl, choose a sipper water bottle that hangs from the outside of their cage.

THE LITTER BOX

Rabbits like to have one or two places to poop. You will want a litter box for the cage and one for the pen. It's easy to set up a litter box. You need a litter pan, a rack, bunny-safe **absorbent** litter, and hay.

Put some absorbent litter material in the bottom of the pan and set the rabbit rack on top. Then, place a bunch of hay on the rack. Your rabbits will sit comfortably on the hay and poop while they munch away! Be sure to clean the tray daily to keep urine odors away.

Using a rack to separate hay from the litter helps to keep your rabbit's hay clean and dry.

SNUGGLE BUNNIES

Because rabbits have soft, smooth fur, you will definitely want to snuggle with them. Snuggling is fine, but you need to learn the proper way to cuddle up to your friends.

Most rabbits frighten easily and do not like it when you pick them up. They squirm and kick their back legs. They may accidentally break their fragile backs in a struggle. If you must pick them up, give their back feet support. Then, bring them close to your chest.

You want your furry friends to feel safe and secure, and to satisfy their curiosity with you in a natural way. Therefore, the best way to snuggle with your furry friends is to sit on the floor and let them come to you.

Rabbits require the same amount of daily attention as dogs do. Spend at least 30 minutes a day with your rabbits.

BUNNY HEALTH CARE

Pet rabbits need regular checkups from a **veterinarian**. A qualified vet will let you know about their health concerns. For instance, did you know bunnies get hairballs? When rabbits groom, or lick, themselves, they swallow a lot of hair. Their bodies are not able to cough them up, so a diet high in fiber helps your rabbit digest the hair, and a daily brushing helps keep the amount of hair swallowed to a minimum.

Rabbits have sharp nails that can scratch you. Do not remove them. They use their nails for balance. Just have them clipped regularly.

When clipping your rabbit's nails be sure not to cut so close that you expose the quick, which is the fleshy pink vein in the nail.

Rabbit teeth are another concern. Since rabbit teeth never stop growing, a proper diet helps rabbits grind and trim their teeth as they chew. If you see drool or wet hair around their mouths, bring them to the veterinarian for a dental checkup. The vet will also want to see your bunnies if you notice changes in their eating, drinking, or litter box habits.

If you put the proper time and patience into raising your pet rabbits, you will find that they make wonderful pets.

KNOW YOUR RABBITS!

Angora

Himalayan

Holland Lop

Lion-Head

Netherland Dwarf

New Zealand

GLOSSARY

absorbent (ab-ZOR-buhnt): able to soak up liquid

domestic (duh-MESS-tik): no longer wild

isolated (EYE-suh-layt-ed): alone or separated

neutering (NOO-tur-ing): surgically removing the reproductive organs in a male animal

pellets (PEL-ets): small, hard balls or tubes

predators (PRED-uh-turz): animals that hunt other animals for food

spaying (SPAY-ing): surgically removing the reproductive organs in a female animal

supplement (SUHP-luh-muhnt): to add something

veterinarian (vet-ur-uh-NAIR-ee-un): a person trained to treat injured or sick animals

Index

Websites

www.bunnyrabbits.org/

www.humanesociety.org/animals/rabbits/

www.thebunnybasics.com

petrabbitcare.org/

About the Authors

David and Patricia Armentrout live near Cincinnati, Ohio, with their two sons and dog, Max. After adopting Max in 2001, it didn't take long before he won over the hearts of family, friends, and neighbors! The Armentrouts have also had other pets over the years, including cats, birds, guinea pigs, snakes, fish, turtles, frogs, and hermit crabs.